"You don't marry the person you can live with,
you marry the person you can't live without."

Unknown

The BIG Wedding Planner

Everything you need to know (but didn't)

Happiness cannot be far behind
a grateful heart
and a peaceful mind

(Anon)

The author has made every effort to ensure
the accuracy of all quotations
Unless otherwise stated, photographs are courtesy of Unsplash.com

Contact information: www.maldenandwilde.com

Published by Malden and Wilde
www.maldenandwilde.com

Contents

Welcome Lovely Ladies!

I am your BIG Wedding Planner!

Your essential wedding toolkit for everything you need for your big day

I will be your companion, information point and security blanket when you can't remember details, or appointments, or feel like chucking it all in because of overwhelm!

And now ....

While that first wonderful excitement lasts – take time to just enjoy being engaged to each other! Wedding planning is - and always should be – exciting and fun. It can also sometimes feel like WORK! So just for a moment – feel that magic!

Ready?

Let's do this!

In the book which is my memory
On the first page of the chapter that is the day when I first met you
Appear the words 'Here begins a new life'

Dante Alighieri

The Essentials

Your Wedding Outfit

Your choice, your style - always!

Right, lovely ladies!

Talk to any bride and she'll tell you that choosing your wedding dress is always the biggest deal. 'You will know when you find THE DRESS' is a common mantra – but what if you don't?

And what if you don't want a traditional wedding dress? Would a cocktail dress, tea dress or a snappy trouser suit be ok? For sure!

Here are my top tips ....

TOP TIPS

Know your venue and theme from the start – and use your common sense. For example, a light floaty dress would be easier to manage in a woodland setting in the heat of summer, than a heavy brocade dress with a long train.

Know your own personal style. Confidence is everything. Let's face it, most models are size 6 or 8 (or less) and most of us are not! And that fabulous dress on Pinterest may not suit you! If you are a curvy bride, how does that outfit make you feel? Do you feel a bit vulnerable or sensational? And if a snappy suit is more your thing – make sure it fits beautifully in every way, and that you feel both comfortable and confident wearing it.

Don't look at the size label! Dresses tend to be cut smaller than you would expect. You may find you are trying on dresses that, according to the label, are a couple of sizes bigger than your usual dress size. All that matters is whether you like it, it suits you and the price is right.

and there's more .....

Charlotte is the owner of Maisie Darling Bridal Boutique in Lutterworth, Leicestershire
She is a confessed shoe addict, and has the happiest smile!

Here are Charlotte's TOP TIPS when you are dress shopping

Different silhouettes highlight different parts of the body. Try a variety of different ones to find the perfect type for you.
It may not be the one you thought it would be!

Putting on a pair of shoes (doesn't have to be your ACTUAL wedding shoes) during your appointment will help to see the dress differently. As you are walking around the boutique (or swooshing!) shoes will alter the way you stand and hold your body

However, try to be open minded with the dress styles you try on, as you are then much more likely to find the perfect dress for you. Always try the wildcard!

Dress shopping is an exciting and momentous experience. But it can be very confusing if you have too many opinions! Ideally bring 2 people with you who will consider you and your style.

Try and consider what undies to wear to your appointment. First of all, it will help your confidence. If you have a pair of knickers that have a big hole in the back, you won't feel very glamourous! Secondly try to wear nude or light colours. The appearance of a dress will be totally different if your green polka dot bra is on show!

Your Budget

Before you begin trying on outfits, work out what your budget is. Include your veil if you choose to have one, shoes and accessories. Your dress will be the big ticket item.

Don't be tempted into buying fabulous £300 shoes with killer heels that you will probably never wear again. You may not be able to wear them all day without pain!

Accessories may include jewellery, a wrist corsage, and bridal crown which can be jewelled or floral (or none of these things – keeping it simple is ok too!).

Try and factor in the cost of any alterations ….

And don't forget your underwear ….

TOP TIP : Take your Bride's Bestie Personal Practical Planner (or a notebook) with you. You may have 'information overload' and not recall the best details of your top picks, so jotting things down will be invaluable.

Tag photos on your phone with any info you need to help you remember.

Notes

Photo: Emma DB Photography

The Veil

Your choice, your style - always!

Wearing a veil is a very old tradition. The bride wears the veil over her face to ward off evil spirits.

The veil completes the beautiful and romantic image of the blushing bride. However, many brides wear a simple circlet of flowers matching the bouquet, with all the romantic symbolism that can have.

Does having a veil feel a bit OTT? You can buy some stunning hair accessories that are hand crafted – pins, hair vines and tiaras of all shapes and styles. The simple elegant statement is just as beautiful as that gorgeous cathedral veil!

Veil?   Yes/No   Flower Crown?   Yes/No

Sparkly tiara?   Yes/No

Notes

I still have my feet on the ground. I just wear better shoes

Oprah Winfrey

Your wedding shoes

What is YOUR style? Flats? Sparkly sneakers? Statement heels?

Do you wear six inch heels at work? How do you feel at the end of the day? Does your back ache?
Do your ankles and knees ache? Bear this in mind when shopping for wedding shoes.

High heels are beautifully elegant and really flattering to the leg and ankle. They complement and complete the over-all look of fabulousness! Again, comfort is key.

Choose your statement shoes with the heel height that you are most accustomed to wearing, or that you feel you can wear all day without pain.

CHECK the season
Remember that in hot weather, your feet will naturally swell, so be careful about buying close fitting shoes for a summer wedding; they may pinch and give you blisters on a hot day. Leather shoes will fare better than satin if you have to walk anywhere in wet or damp weather.

CHECK your Venue
Highly polished or stone floors at your venue or church. These can be slippery. Make sure you know what to expect before you buy your shoes.

CHECK your Budget
Lovely bride Claire's advice is don't worry too much about your wedding shoes. They won't be seen and the most important thing is that they are comfortable.

Notes

Perfume

A very personal choice. Your perfume aligns with your personality in wonderfully subtle ways.

Things to bear in mind ….
- Keep it light for a summer wedding.
- Make sure that your partner loves it too – and that it won't clash with whatever scent or perfume they are planning wearing!

Accessories

- Jewellery – think about the style of your dress or outfit. Earrings, graceful back-drape necklaces for those naked backs, bridal bracelet – as with everything, it's what fits with your personality and style. (An heirloom necklace is a sweet way of acknowledging loved ones.)
- Hair Accessories – tiara, pretty hair pins, floral comb or crown (with real or silk flowers)
- Shawl or wrap – Lovely for a boho look; faux fur jackets for a winter wedding or beautiful warm shawls
- My tip – keep it simple. Your accessories are part of the background to your beautiful picture

Notes

Your Hair Stylist

Lorna is an award winning hairstylist with her salon in Sharnbrook, Bedfordshire. She always has a cheery smile and a warm welcome.

HER TOP TIPS

- Before deciding on your hairstyle, pick your dress or outfit. If you have longer hair, you may prefer an updo if the back of your dress is a beautiful feature.

- Check your hair colour. Bright blondes can look washed out with white dresses. Cream is better, but if you've set your heart on white, don't worry. Talk to your hairstylist about a rinse to soften your colour

- Usually, you will need to book 4 – 6 months ahead. But it's always a good idea to have that informal conversation with your hairdresser when you are newly engaged – and ask then when would be a good time to book her.

- Have your hair trials, with your hair accessories and veil, on the same day as your dress fitting – so you can get a real snapshot of how it will all look.

and there's more .....

- Wash your hair the day before your wedding. This will mean that it will be more manageable for your hairdresser to arrange into that stunning style without too much freshly washed silkiness.

- Be aware of the timings of the day. If your hairdresser comes to your home or where you are getting ready, it could take longer than in the salon, as there are always distractions to hold things up.

- Get the foundations of your make up done before your hair. Your makeup artist will use a soft ring to keep your hair away from your face while she works so no product is transferred.

TIP FOR YOUR CHIEF BRIDESMAID
Make sure she has a travel bag with hair spray and extra hair pins as precautions against those odd breezes and wisps of hair escaping when they're not supposed to.

The last week before your wedding will be manic – take time to relax and just be with your partner!

Notes

Photo: Emma DB Photography

Your Bridal Make Up

Bridal makeup can give you a great confidence boost, especially as the chances are you will be tired from the planning and excitement. This shows in your skin and features.

When you have makeup professionally done, it makes a difference to the quality of your photographs. It looks very different compared with "day to day" makeup.

Here are my top tips

FIND AN ARTIST WHOSE STYLE YOU LIKE
Social media is your friend here, plus get recommendations from friends and family. With something so personal, it's important that you get on with and trust your stylist

BE REALISTIC with your expectations.
The best way to choose a look you want to go for, is going through the artist's own work. Pinterest is great for getting ideas but they may not suit your face shape or skin tone.

GET A TRIAL and trust your artist's advice.
Trials are important because they can rule out anything you are not sure about. When you have had your trial, try to keep the makeup on all day and see how it wears through the day and in photographs. How does your skin feel the next day? Give your artist feedback so she can adjust the product she uses to get the best result for you

Make sure she has the timings of your day to ensure she has enough time to work

Notes

The Rings

Choosing your rings

Choosing your rings should be exciting, romantic (make it an event!) – with a dose of common sense thrown in. Have fun together and make it part of the excitement, not the stress!

Your Style, Your lifestyle, your choice

From The KNOT:
"Choose something that represents you because these pieces truly become a part of you, and commonly become heirlooms that are cherished and passed down to future generations," says Alex Stuller, senior director of bridal at ever&ever

Set a budget and stick to it

Easy to get swept up by a beautiful set only to find that you can't actually afford it! (Some websites recommend estimates of 3% - 5% of your total wedding budget.) Prices actually vary a lot from one retailer to another, depending on the metal you choose, the width of the rings and whether or not you have diamonds added. Shopping around is always a good idea!

What metal should you choose?

Cost, your skin tone and any allergies all play their part. Bear in mind that some metals scratch more easily than others – your lifestyle may dictate which metal you choose!

According to Cleveland Clinic (www.health.clevelandclinic.org) the most common metal allergies are to nickel, cobalt and chromates which manufacturers often use to alloy with other metals. Metals less likely to cause a reaction are copper, yellow gold, platinum, stainless steel adn sterling silver.

The recommendation is to avoid white gold and plated metals as these are often plated with nickel

Popular metals for wedding rings

TITANIUM is a lightweight metal with a lustrous grey appearance. It is very strong and durable and has become increasingly popular with couples as a less expensive, but still beautiful, alternative to platinum or gold.

PLATINUM: This white-coloured metal is extremely tough and stands up well to everyday wear and tear. It's rarer than gold and much more expensive but a platinum wedding ring will last, unmarked, forever.

PALLADIUM is a very rare metal in the platinum group of metals and looks very similar in colour to platinum but is much less dense. This means it is a great choice if you want the steely white colour of platinum but not the weight on your finger. It is now cherished for its lustrous silvery-white finish and because of its similar properties to platinum. Palladium is resistant to corrosion and will not tarnish in air. It is relatively hard-wearing and does not require plating.
(from weddingrings-direct.com)

YELLOW GOLD Choose 14 or 18 carat. 22carat is too soft for wedding rings that will have constant wear of a long period of time.

WHITE GOLD is often plated with RHODIUM which wears off – my daughter had to get hers re-plated twice to restore it to its original beauty. Worth paying a bit more for something that will last!

The Rings continued

Sizing

Remember that your fingers swell in the heat and shrink a bit in the cold. You can't plan for every eventuality; use your common sense as well as taking the advice of your jeweller. Resizing could be an option should it prove to be necessary nearer the day.

Shop early

Six months in advance is a good idea for bespoke rings.

If you find the rings you both love, you will need a few weeks to have the rings delivered and checked.

And lastly ......

Consider wedding insurance

Add your rings – wedding and engagement - to your household insurance. Just in case.
(My son in law lost his wedding ring in the sea. Just saying…)

Notes

Your Bridesmaids

There is no rule that says you have to have bridesmaids.

You might opt for flower girls...

You don't have to choose all your girl friends and female relatives either.

MY TOP TIPS

CHECK YOUR BUDGET

In the UK, you will be expected to pay for your bridesmaids' dresses. This could help you decide how many bridesmaids and/or flower girls to have.

For hair and makeup, shoes and accessories, it's reasonable to expect them to pay for their own – but make sure that they know this in advance.

MAKE A LIST

Of who you're closest to, who will cheer you on, who you know you can rely on to support you and not make the wedding about them. Include close relatives – sisters, sisters-in-law, nieces.. (do you get on with them?) but don't get pressured into agreeing to more distant rellies who you barely know

Bridemaids Top Tips continued

Beware of premature requests with all the excitement of getting engaged.

That party-animal gal could be a nightmare, much as you love her!

Take your time!

When in doubt – keep it simple!

If you decide to have only flower girls or young bridesmaids (aged 9 – 11, say) no adults can be offended.

Same with keeping to relatives.

Friends who pout about not being asked ….
Need I say more?

Decide on your Chief Bridesmaid or Maid of Honour (men are not excluded!)

This person must be reliable, help you with choosing your outfit, willing to prop you up when you're having a wobble, sort out your hen party (and hold your head up when you're being sick), and get your dress out of the way when you're going to the loo.

Photo: Emma DB Photography

What does your Chief Bridesmaid do?

WEDDING OUTFIT SHOPPING

Be supportive when you're having a wobble, give you her honest opinion (gently put, in need!), help you think outside the box when it's called for.

PLAN THE HEN PARTY

Liaise with you to check who should be invited, who can go, budgets of invitees, where and when.

Then organise the fun date for about three months before the wedding. Don't forget taxis home so everyone can relax and not worry about driving with alcohol.

ORGANISE THE BRIDESMAIDS

- Discuss with you whether or not they should pay for their own dresses, accessories, hair and makeup, and make sure the bridesmaids are aware.
- Sort out dress shopping dates, appointments booked, lunch organised and so on.
- Make sure the bridesmaids know when and where they have to be on the big day.

SUPPORT YOU WITH ANY PLANNING

This is entirely up to you as a couple – but your Chief Bridesmaid could help you brainstorm ideas, colour themes, addressing invitation envelopes, sorting out who has replied to invitations, and so on.

She should have your back and be cheerful, willing to help, and equally willing to back off and not take offence if you don't want her assistance!

What the Chief Bridesmaid does

On the Big Day

- Make sure that you have breakfast – even if you feel too wired to eat. Trust me. You will be glad she did! Your Chief Bridesmaid should also make sure you eat and drink at the reception – so much excitement, so much going on, it's easy to forget!

- Take delivery of flowers and make sure everyone has the right bouquet or corsage.

- Give you any help you need while you get ready.

- Greet the photographer and make sure he knows where, who and when he has to do his shots.

- Make sure that everyone in the bridal party leaves in good time to get to the ceremony at least ten minutes before you.

Have a Bride Emergency Kit ready

Lots of tissues! Plasters for blisters, spare hair pins, deodorant, hair spray, needle and thread, makeup repair – like moist cotton pads for streaking mascara from tears, lipstick etc

Flower girls

Flowers girls (aged 4 – 7) and perhaps 'junior'
bridesmaids (aged 9 - 14)
can add fun and cuteness to your day

- Choose your own little girl, if you have one (of course!), your nieces or your partner's, or both, keeping everything in the family. Your closest friends won't then wonder why their little darlings haven't been chosen as flower girls.
- If you are a bit short on young female relatives, consider the daughters of your best friends, especially if you are also wanting their mums to be bridesmaids.

What flowers do they carry?
Little flower girls don't actually need to have anything to hold – they can hold hands! However, a little basket of flowers or a wand (fairy or flower) will add to the cute factor. Of course, even very little girls like to feel important and having a wand or basket to match the bride will do the trick!

The little details
Again, these are dependant on your budget. A circlet of flowers, or a dainty beaded headdress can be a lovely and very personal accessory for both flower girls and junior bridesmaids.

Notes

Notes

Your Venue

When do you want to get married?

By far and away the most popular months are April through to August.

May, June, September and October are statistically the driest months and also the most popular for choosing your wedding venue.

Late autumn or winter weddings may be dry and frosty – and TOP TIP – venues may charge less than during the peak wedding season

TOP TIP
Book your venue before you start booking your other suppliers, including your church, Registrar or celebrant.

How far in advance do I have to book my venue?

Couples book their venue at least a year in advance of the date, and, post pandemic, may now need to consider two years advance booking. Popular venues may be taking booking as much as three years in advance.

The season will also make a difference when choosing your venue. There are more likely to be long waiting lists for venues during the summer months which are the height of the wedding season.

If you are planning an autumn or winter wedding, be aware that there are peak times where parties are booked up really early. Halloween, Christmas and New Year festivities are all pressure points.

Essential questions to ask before booking

Make a list of what you want before you start.
Set your minimum and maximum budget limits for the venue,
and whether you are going for a DIY/dry hire or want the venue to do everything

- What dates are available? Is your preferred date free?

  ....

- How many guests can the venue seat?

  ....

- Is there accommodation for guests and, if so, how many?

  ....

- Is there disabled access?

  ....

- What is the price?

  ....

- Are there different packages?

  ....

- Is VAT included in the price?

  ....

What's included? (catering, wine, tables and chairs plus set up and tables laid with crockery, cutlery, glassware etc, service charge, staffing, waiter service, MD, DJ, wedding coordinator, accommodation, getting-ready suite)

....

....

....

....

....

- What deposit is required and when?   ....

- Is it non-refundable?   ....

- When is the balance due?   ....

- Is a payment plan available?   ....

....

....

- Is the venue licensed to hold religious and/or civil ceremonies?

....

- Are there any restrictions? Such as Local regs that mean the party has to end at midnight esp for an outdoors reception, no-go areas, access time limits for florist and event décor set up and take down.

....

....

....

- Parking for bridal party and guests?

....

- Wet weather provision if the reception is outside?

....

- Rustic settings with teepees – are they included in the costs? What about toilet facilities?

....

....

- When does the venue need numbers, dietary requirements etc?

....

....

- Can the date be moved if the church/celebrant/registrar isn't available?

....

- Does the venue have liability insurance?

....

- Are you and your guests covered for accidents or injuries on the day?

....

- What's the venue's cancellation policy?

....

....

....

....

....

Who will be our specific contact person at the venue?

....

....

Notes

Catering

Essential Questions to ask your Caterer

- Are you free?

....

- Do you cater more than one wedding a day?

....

- Are you familiar with our venue? If not, provide the name and contact details of your liaison person.

....

....

- What food do you offer?

....

- Are specialisms, children's menu, diabetic, vegan, kosher or halal catered for?

....

- Can we order meals for other suppliers, like DJ and photographer?

....

- How do you charge? Per head or per function? Does this include VAT?

....

Catering

Essential Questions continued

- What can you show us? Do you offer a tasting menu?

  ....

- Can we see your reviews?

  ....

- Where do you source your ingredients? Do you use local providers?

  ....

- Cutting up the cake for distribution to guests – do you do this and do you charge?

  ....

- Do you provide waiters? How many?

  ....

- For dry hire/DIY weddings, do you provide tables, chairs, linen, crockery, glassware, cutlery etc?

  ....

- Can you supply equipment for outdoor receptions like lights, generators etc if the venue doesn't provide them?

  ....

- Do you provide cocktails, champagne for toasts, wine on the tables, champagne and canapes as guests arrive, water on tables, kids' drinks?

  ....

Catering

Essential Questions continued

- What access do you need to the venue and how long do you need to set up?

  ....

  ....

- Do you clear up at the end of the function?

  ....

- Do you dispose of waste – food, half empty bottles, breakages etc

  ....

- When do you need numbers and final menu choices?

  ....

- What is your cancellation policy?

....

....

Notes

Your Seating Plan

First thing to remember.

All your guests are there because they love and care about you both and want you to be happy. Plus everyone knows what the situation is so they are likely to be reasonable. Even the awkward customers who get bolshie when they've had a few! So try not to stress too much. You can only do what you can, and the rest – having fun, being sociable, cheering you on – is down to them.

Your venue can help you

Have a chat with your wedding coordinator about how many tables they can accommodate. Will they be round or long? Seating will be generally around a metre apart, so a 10ft round table will comfortably accommodate 6 - 8 people.

Long tables can seat guests in a zigzag pattern or with guests only along one side. Perhaps in a horseshoe arrangement with everyone looking inward?

Your Seating Plan continued

So who sits where?

Top Table
Bride and Bride, parents, Chief Bridesmaid

Guests
All sorts of combinations – and none – are possible.

BEST TIP - Group your guests per table. For example family, friends, work colleagues, friends of parents, and so on. As far as possible, make sure that everyone knows someone at the table. Avoid having a 'singles' table unless they all happen to be friends, and try not to have one loner on a table of couples.

Consider having a kids' table, if warranted.

You could assign people to tables rather than actual seats. Place names won't be needed, but waiting staff could find it tricky, especially if specific diets have to be accommodated.

It can be a good idea to consult parents about their friends and who should go where.

Notes

Photo: Emma DB Photography

Arranging your wedding decor

First of all, decide what sort of wedding you want - DIY or with the help of a wedding coordinator. Or somewhere in between

DIY

- Rope in family and friends early on – it's fun to craft your own decorations, table arrangements, chair decorations and so on.
- Allocate tasks on the day so that you can relax and concentrate on getting ready.
- Make sure everyone knows the timings for setting up and clearing away.
- Check with your venue if there is anyone who will be on hand on the day to solve any problems that may arise.

YOUR FLORIST

Your florist may offer to do floral installations at the venue, table décor, flowers for the cake table, flowers for the ceremony and so on. Make sure that the venue knows who they will be dealing with, and that access times are clear.

WEDDING COORDINATOR

- Your venue may provide a coordinator who can liaise with your florist or event designer and take charge for you – major stress buster!
- Make sure the coordinator knows what you want and how you want everything to look. Having detailed conversations will be helpful, mapping things out, brainstorming alternatives where necessary, including anything you create yourself and so on.

EVENT STYLIST

This is someone who sorts out reception décor, table décor, chair décor (ribbons, sashes, little floral arrangements etc), and may also be able to provide extras like arches,special table settings and so on. Like the florist, communication with the venue will be key to a smooth, trouble-free set up.

Notes

The DJ and entertainment

Here are some great tips from limelightentertainmentnj.com

Let their qualifications, not your relationship (best mate, favourite uncle), be the determining factor. This should be an arrangement like any other wedding supplier so make sure that you are in a contract that specifically spells out your obligations and theirs!

CONTRACT. This is essential. It should detail a rough idea of timings (so you know if there are extra charges past a certain time), requirements for the day, and cancellation fees.
It's something that works both ways. Once you've signed their contract you've committed to using them, so any DJ who doesn't offer you a contract should set alarm bells ringing.

Who do people recommend? Read reviews to find out why. Do you know someone who had an awesome DJ?

Personality – are they your sort of person? Do they love what they do – or seem a bit jaded? The DJ plays an important part in making the reception a happy place, and if you have any doubts at all, (even the niggly ones that seems petty), walk away!

Make sure they can correctly pronounce all the names in the wedding party.

Make a short-list of DJs and interview them. If a DJ won't make time for an interview, how likely is he or she to make time for you during the wedding planning

Questions to ask your DJ

- What's your experience and style?

  ....

- Are you available for our date?

  ....

- When do we need to book?

  ....

- What do you charge? Hourly or by event?

  ....

- What does it include? Set up and take down time? Overtime? Wifi mics?

  ....

  ....

- What is NOT included?

  ....

....

....

- How long will you play for?

....

- How many weddings do you do in a weekend?

....

- Have you played at our venue?

....

- Can we give you a 'do not play' list?

....

- What is the deposit you need?

....

- What is your cancellation/refund policy?

....

....

- What do you do in the event of illness etc? Do you have a backup DJ who can step in?

....

....

- What special arrangements do you need? Eg power outlets, position and space, timing for set up, wifi, meals etc

....

....

Notes

....

....

....

....

....

....

....

....

....

....

Choosing your flowers and your florist

Imagine your wedding is a blank canvas, with you and your partner in the centre of the frame.
Your colour scheme will be the background and the flowers will complete the design

YOUR BUDGET

Statistically, couples spend approximately 10% of their total wedding budget on their bridal flowers and 10% on their decor. You will be looking at between £700 and £1500 for your flowers as a minimum, depending on the size of the wedding. This could include those for the ceremony or church, bridesmaids and flower girls, and buttonholes/corsages. There is, however, a global shortage of flowers post-pandemic, and this is likely to continue for a number of years. You can expect prices to rise!

YOUR COLOUR SCHEME AND STYLE

What do you have in mind? A relaxed boho style? Country chic? Classic formal?

Think of your story … when did you get your first bouquet? what's your favourite perfume? are some flowers part of your family's story? Granny's favourite, maybe? Pressed flowers found in an old book of poems that tell a story?

When you go to the supermarket and reach a bunch of flowers… what do you go for? Scent? Certain flowers? Colour? and, most of all, why?

CHOOSING YOUR FLORIST
Word of mouth is always a good way of finding a florist who will give you excellent service and stunning results, so ask your friends. Is there a florist who is local to your venue? Does your venue recommend a florist? Create a shortlist of florists and, if time allows, make appointments to see them all. Look through their portfolios, and get a sense of their expertise.

TOP TIP –
Do you like the florist as a person? Working closely with someone who makes you feel uncomfortable will only add to your stress! Sometimes, small is better! Your local florist will give a really personal service and allocate the time needed exclusively to you.

Once you've decided on your florist, tell her your story and your vision. You can show her your Pinterest boards, maybe swatches or sketches of your dress and the dresses of your bridesmaids. Talk about your table plans, whether they will be round or long, as this will impact on the sort of table décor you have

TOP TIP: Thinking about faux flowers?
Don't assume that they will be cheaper than fresh flowers. High quality silk flowers are realistic and are as expensive as fresh flowers. They are an investment as you will keep them for years!

Questions to ask your florist

- Are you available on our date?

  ....

- Are you familiar with our venue?

  ....

- Can we choose our flowers? Are our favourite flowers in season?

  ....

- How long have you been a florist?

  ....

- When do we book? Will we be the priority on the day?

  ....

- How many weddings do you do in a month?

  ....

- Do you use locally grown flowers? Are you eco-friendly?

  ....

- What is your deposit? When is it payable? Is it refundable?

  ....

  ....

- Do you have a minimum spend?

  ....

- What does your price include?

....

....

- Do you offer sample arrangements?

....

- What is NOT included (VAT, delivery, extra time spent at the ceremony and venue etc)

....

....

- Can you work within our budget?

....

- Do you have a contract?

....

- What is your cancellation/refund policy?

....

....

....

Notes

Notes

Notes

Photo: smileyhuseyinphotography.com

Choosing your Cake

Sounds like a no-brainer but …..Always ask your cake designer for advice, they are the experts! Heidi and Angie of Simply Irresistible Cakes of London create the most amazing designs!

Heidi's Top Tips

What sort of cake?
Consider these…..

- What type of wedding are you having? Formal affair in a grand venue or a relaxed intimate venue? or have you chosen to go a bit more rustic?
- The time of year you are getting married and the practicalities of that. For example, a buttercream covered cake in a marquee in mid August when it's really hot, could lead to disaster. (enter sagging cake and melting buttercream!)
- How many guests will be you having and how you will be serving the cake? (will it be the dessert after your meal or will it be served with coffee/evening buffet?)

Is cake very important to you?
Do you want it to be a centrepiece and talking point of the day and beyond!?

Discuss with your planner or venue coordinator where the cake table will be placed (preferably not in a dingy corner!)

Your Budget
How much do you want to spend on your cake? For example, a cake that has lots of sugar flowers will cost considerably more than a semi-naked cake with fresh flowers.

Choosing your Cake continued

Be realistic.

Remember that wedding cakes take many hours of work, often 3-5 days, so do take this into consideration. Don't believe the "average" price for a wedding cake that you may see written in many places. Wedding cakes are anything but average!

Tasting – the fun part!!

Can you have different flavours in each tier? Yes, you can! Most cake designers do cake taster boxes or have tasters available during your consultation. Note: there is often a charge for this and it's usually stated on the designer's website.

Choosing your designer

- Do a little online research. Look for someone either local to you or to the venue (who will also usually have a recommended supplier list). Look at their reviews and the work displayed on their website/social media. Do they make the types of cakes that you are drawn to?
- Visit a wedding fair and have a chat to the cake designers there. Did you 'click' with any of them? Did they give you confidence? Did they come up with some good suggestions?

and there's more ...

Choosing your Cake continued

Sending that first email to a cake designer

Cake by Silverleaf Cake Company

- In the first instance, it's important to include your wedding date and venue, so that they can check their availability.
- Then offer as much detail as you can – number of guests, styles of cakes that you like, how you are going to serve the cake etc. It will speed up the process and make it much easier for you with fewer emails back and forth!
- I believe that you can get a 'feel' for a person from emails, so make sure you are happy with their responses. You want to feel confident!

Every designer runs their business differently, but most offer consultations with tasters either online or in person. Be sure to attend one and check you are happy with everything. Then book your designer with a booking fee and you are sorted!

Happy cake searching!

Notes

Your Photographer

Emma Drew Batty is a talented photographer who always goes the extra mile to provide a stunning selection of photographs

Emma's Top Tips

Shop around! Always arrange to meet up before you decide. Don't settle on the first person you talk to, even if you feel stressed out by the whole process and have information overload. When all the excitement is over, your wedding photos will remain and it's so important to make sure they are done properly and will continue to give you pleasure long after the event.

1
Have a checklist of what you are looking for in a photographer – style, experience, price, delivery

What is the photographer's style and length of experience?
Don't be afraid to ask! Any photographer confident in their work and ability will be able to show you!

Emma's Top Tips continued

2
Trust their judgement about the shot list.
You don't need to have a huge list. Your photographer will have this covered.

Can specific shots be taken? If not, will they work to your own shot list? Communication is key. Make sure you understand exactly what the photographer has in mind and that you like it.

3
Timings of the day

Make sure that your photographer knows well in advance what the timings of the day are, so they can take bridal prep shots, pre-ceremony shots, first look shots, and so on.

4
How to choose?

Get recommendations from your venue and other suppliers, as well as from friends and family.

5
What if it rains?

Enjoy it! Rain brings good luck, and umbrella photos can be fun!

Questions to ask your photographer continued

- What are our rights as the customer? [Remember that copyright will be with the photographer but you should have lifelong rights of use.]

....

....

- What about use of your photos on social media? Is this limited in any way?

....

- What arrangements will you make to ensure our wedding is covered in the event of accident or illness?

....

....

- Do you have insurance?

....

- What is your cancellation/refund policy, including if the wedding is cancelled or postponed?

....

- Do you have a contract?

....

[This is essential to protect your investment and guard against cowboys! The contract should set out clear expectations, covering terms of payment, deposits, delivery and when the final payment is due. Make sure you read the small print...]

Questions to ask your photographer

- How many weddings will you be shooting on the same day? Will there be a second shooter/assistant?

   ....

   ....

- When will you start taking photos?

   ....

- How many hours will your contract allow for?

   ....

- Will you ask the ceremony and reception venues about their photo protocols?

   ....

- Have you photographed a wedding at our venue before?

   ....

   ....

Finally..... what is a good deal?

Investment in gear is expensive and post processing and compilation of images is a time consuming process, especially if books are involved.' If the deal sounds too good to be true, it probably is!

Notes

Photo: Emma DB Photography

Wedding Cars

Top Tips

Before booking wedding cars, there are a number of things to consider ...
Do you have to hire cars? No - if you have friends or relatives who have lovely cars that they are happy for you to use on the day. Provided, of course, that the cars are reliable, and that you will have someone to drive you

If you are using a wedding car company.....

- See the car first, so you know what you're getting and you can be sure of the colour, style and condition
- Can you sit down in your dress or outfit? Can you get into the car easily?
- Is the car company part of the National Association of Wedding Car Professionals? Look for the logo as security that you are not dealing with a cowboy or scammer
- Book in plenty of time – cars get booked up early specially for the summer months
- How will bridesmaids and senior members of the bridal party get to the venue? Will you need extra cars?

Top Tips

What is the average cost of wedding car hire?

On average, car hire is around £200. There are regional variations, plus the price varies according to the type of car and the length of journeys to the ceremony and then to venue

When does the couple have to arrive at the ceremony?

How closely you follow tradition is your choice. Will you walk down the aisle together? or will one of you walk towards the other? Whatever you decide, get to the ceremony no later than 15 minutes beforehand.

Who travels with whom?

Traditionally, the Bride and her father will travel in one car to the ceremony.
The Mother of the Bride and bridesmaids will travel together
However, it's YOUR day. Choose whatever combination works for you - and makes sure everyone is where they need to be in good time.

When does everyone else have to arrive?

Ushers: 45 minutes beforehand
Guests: 30 minutes beforehand
Parents: 15 minutes beforehand
Mothers of the couple and Bridesmaids: 10 minutes beforehand
Fathers of the Brides: 5 minutes beforehand
(NB: If you are having pre-ceremony photographs at the church or temple,
make sure you allow for the time needed

Wedding Cars continued

Questions to ask before booking

How do you charge?
eg per seat, per hour, per car

....

Will the distance of the journey affect the cost?

....

How long will we have the cars for?

....

Do all cars come with a driver?

....

What happens if the driver is unwell?

....

Who decorates the car?

....

What deposit will we have to pay?

....

When will we need to pay the final balance?

....

When should we book?

....

What is your cancellation policy?

....

Notes

Your Guest List

When deciding who – and who not – to invite, try to remain practical and pragmatic, keep your budget and maximum numbers in mind – and be kind to folk who question why they weren't invited.

It can be tricky to know who to include, while keeping your budget under control, and so I've devised a formula that could be of help.

Priority Invites + Family Friends + Couple's friends = maximum number of guests

Or you could swop things around

Maximum number of guests → priority invites + family friends + couple's friends

#1 Priority guests

Elderly relatives.

Immediate family – siblings and their partners, parents

Close relatives – emphasis is on the word 'close'

[Keep an eye on your maximum numbers, especially if you have a large extended family.]

2 Family Friends

People who have had a positive influence on your life, who have known you and your family for years.

3 Your friends and their partners

Your Guest List continued

Question – should you invite your boss and colleagues? No – not unless you know them socially. The easiest way to decide is to ask yourself – 'if I changed job, who of my present colleagues would I continue to see in five years time?' Keep office politics away from your wedding.

What about children?
Your wedding is not a kids' party! If you don't want children at your wedding, make it clear, don't apologise for your decision and let your invited guests sort out their baby sitting arrangements.

Communication with Suppliers and Guests

- Create a special wedding email account so your private email account doesn't get clogged up
- Make sure your guests and family know it and use it – they may need reminding!
- Your wedding contact list can also be kept separate from your private one – which could save confusion if you send a blanket email to your contacts and include people who haven't been invited, by mistake.
- Create folders within the account to separate out guest replies and questions, suppliers, family communications and so on.

Make your life as simple as possible!

Notes

Invitations

Top Tips

• Do you really need 'save the date' cards?

Strictly speaking, no. If you have guests who live some distance away and who will need to make special arrangements, or if you are having a destination wedding, sending them early notification will be really helpful and may ensure that these special people are able to attend.

• Have a definite RSVP date specified.
Talk to your venue or caterer to find out their last date for numbers and for your seating plan to be adjusted. For your own peace of mind, two weeks before the date is reasonable.

• Invitations should be sent 4 to 6 months before the date.

If you send out Save the Date cards, send the invitations at least 8 weeks before the date.

• Printed invites or emails?
There is something wonderful and exciting about choosing a design set that matches your theme – even if you are making your own DIY invitations. Emails can save money but may be missed or may not be accessible for older guests.

Invitations

What to include with each invitation

- Information sheet with your invitation: Address and postcode of ceremony venue and reception venue. If necessary, add advice re satnav reliability.

- Dietary requirements: Ask guests to specify if they are vegetarian or have allergies to any foods. This can be emailed back to you or added to the RSVP card

- RSVP card TOP TIP: don't forget to make sure each card/envelope is self-addressed and stamped. You are more likely to get them returned!

If you prefer (and to save costs) give your RSVP email address instead – and remember to keep a check on your spam folder, just in case!

- Dress code: Your choice, but make it clear so no-one feels over-dressed or under-dressed... 'Black tie', 'cocktail attire', 'smart casual', 'casual attire' are all acceptable.

- If you are getting married abroad, include information about available accommodation and transport.

- Create a spreadsheet or other list format of all the invites you send out: names, addresses, emails, phone numbers, relationship (eg best friend's boyfriend/girlfriend)
- Add sections for replies received, attending/not attending, dietary requirements, allergies etc.
- It takes time to set up, but it's time well spent and will save you hours in the end.

Notes

Your Wedding Stationery

Your Style, Your Choice - Always!

What's usually included?

- Save the Date cards (not essential – your choice)
- Invitation and envelopes
- RSVP cards (with stamped addressed envelopes)
- Information sheets
- Orders of Service
- Menu Cards
- Place names (optional)
- Thank you cards (and envelopes)

Before you start looking for a stationer, get your vision clear….

YOUR STYLE
Will your wedding be a relaxed, boho affair or more formal and classic? This can be reflected in the design of your invitations, menu cards, orders of service etc.

YOUR COLOURS
Your colour theme will run through your wedding – bridesmaids' outfits, flowers, décor – everything. They are like the backdrop to your 'portrait' and can reflect who you are. Stuck for ideas? Looking at seasonal colours can help, or the meanings of colours and how they combine.

Your Wedding Stationery continued

Your budget

How much you have allocated to spend on your wedding stationery will have an impact on the design.

Obviously, the more complex the more expensive. When discussing your stationery with your supplier, be upfront about your maximum spend.

TOP TIP: don't forget to factor in postage when you are sorting out your budget!

Shop around

Before settling on your supplier, get recommendations from your venue, other suppliers, family and friends. Order samples! Photos don't always tell the real story and having a sample in your hand could be the game changer!

Questions to ask

- Do you have set packages? What do they include?

....

....

....

- What are the prices?

....

Your Wedding Stationery

Questions to ask continued

- What types of printing do you offer?

  ....

- Do you print in-house or outsource?

  ....

- Do you do custom invitations and stationery?

  ....

- Is there an extra charge for a sample of our custom design?

  ....

- Is there a word limit?

  ....

- Do you offer eco-friendly options for paper and card?

  ....

- How many revisions are included in the package?

  ....

- Is there an extra charge for revisions?

  ....

Your Wedding Stationery

Questions to ask continued

- Will we be sent proofs for checking before signing off the design?

....

- How long does the process take?

....

- When can we expect delivery?

....

- Do you need a deposit?

....

- When is full payment due?

....

- Do you have a contract?

....

- What is your cancellation/refund policy?

....

....

Notes

"There are all types of love in this world, but never the same love twice".
F Scott Fitzgerald

The Ceremony

The Legal Stuff

You can get married in the UK if you are over 16, unmarried and not closely related.
By the way, the rules are slightly different in Scotland and Northern Ireland.
You can check on these websites:
www.mygov.scot/getting-married
www.nidirect.gov.uk/articles/guidance-marriage-procedures-northern-ireland.

Giving notice

- Decide where you want to get married first. If you're having a religious ceremony, before heading off to the Registrar, sort out the date and availability of the church or temple and minister. At the Registrar's Office, you will sign a legal 'notice of intent to get married' that will include where the ceremony is to be held.
- The ceremony must be held with 12 months of registering
- Notice must be given in the district where at least one of you is living.

The Ceremony

The Legal Stuff continued

Civil Partnership or Marriage?

You can choose to have either a religious ceremony or a civil ceremony if you're getting married.

If you're forming a civil partnership you cannot have a religious ceremony. However, same sex couples can convert their civil partnership into a marriage. There is more information at www.gov.uk/convert-civil-partnership

Same-sex couples can get married in a religious building if it has been registered for the marriage of same-sex couples. You cannot get married in an Anglican church as a same-sex couple.

Your vows: You must exchange vows if you're getting married.
You do not need to exchange vows for a civil partnership, but you can if you'd like to.

The Ceremony

Documents you need

- Originals of the following documents to your appointment:
- Details of the final venue for your ceremony
- A valid passport (or UK birth certificate if you were born before 1 January 1983)
- Proof of your home address
- Proof of any name changes (for example, a copy of a deed poll)

To prove your address, bring ONE of the following:

- Valid UK or Irish driving licence
- Gas, water or electricity bill from the last 3 months
- Bank or building society statement from the last month
- Council Tax bill from the last 12 months
- Mortgage statement from the last 12 months
- Current tenancy agreement
- Letter from your landlord (dated within the last 7 days) confirming you live there and including your landlord's name, address and their signature
- If you've been married before, you'll also need to provide either your divorce decree absolute or the death certificate of your late partner.

(source: www.gov.uk/marriages-civil-partnerships/documents-youll-need-to-give-notice)

The Ceremony

The Legal Stuff continued

No-one's life is totally straight forward, so it's always worth checking the government website for the rules and regulations to avoid any hassles later on. And of course, ask your minister or your local Registry Office for guidance.

CIVIL CEREMONIES
All sorts of venues are licensed to hold civil ceremonies, and the law has changed to allow religious ceremonies to be held outdoors within the grounds of the church or temple building.

Of course, you can have the legal marriage ceremony with a Marriage Registrar, followed by a ceremony, with your own vows, officiated by a celebrant who doesn't have to be licensed and can be your favourite uncle.
And this can be held anywhere from a forest glade to a hot air balloon!

REGISTRAR OR CELEBRANT
The person conducting the ceremony must be licensed to do so.

There are celebrants who are licensed as marriage officers and can help you design your own beautiful and unique ceremony and will guide you when you are writing your vows as to what legally must be included.

The Ceremony

The Legal Stuff continued

MAKE IT PERSONAL

There are many creative ways you can add a personal moment to your ceremony too. For thousands of years we've added rituals and symbolism to ceremonies to add more meaning, from the simplicity of lighting a candle to represent the start of a new beginning, to using sand blending to celebrate a new family unity.

FIND YOUR CELEBRANT
https://www.thecelebrantdirectory.com

SIGNING THE REGISTER

The traditional signing of the Marriage Register is no more. But don't despair: that lovely moment can still be captured as the couple has to sign a 'marriage schedule' or 'marriage document' at the ceremony before two witnesses.

The document is then sent to the Registry Office for the marriage to be formally registered and for the marriage certificate to be issued.

I recommend getting several copies. You never know when you might need them in the years ahead!

Notes

Your Vows

Wedding vows in the presence of witnesses and civil registration are a legal requirement. This is because, ultimately, the act of marriage is a binding contract with technicalities for both parties.

All marriage vows have to include a form of words that meet the legal requirements:

- I declare that I know of no legal reason why I (your name) may not be joined in marriage to (your partner's name).
- I (your full name), take you (your partner's full name) to be my wedded wife

The couple can then, with the permission and approval of the Registrar, Celebrant or Minister, speak their own vows to each other.

Here are my top tips

- Whatever you pledge, no matter how skilful you may be with words – and some folk are better at this than others – what you say will come from the heart. Words are just words. It is the sincerity and love behind them that gives them meaning.

- Keep sentences fairly short – they are easier to remember. Simple words, sincerely expressed are incredibly powerful. If you dry up and can't remember what you've written, just speak from the heart!

My Top Tips

- Your vows should take about one minute to say. Practice saying them out loud. Try not to speak too fast. Remember nerves will make you speak more quickly anyway. How do they sound? do you stumble over some of the words? If you are anxious that you will forget what you want to say, print them out on cue cards. Your chief bridesmaid or best man to keep for you until the moment comes. Or keep them in your pocket.

- Just as marriage and living together are part of a unique partnership, working out your vows together is a good idea and can help with nerves on the day. Of course, you could add in your own special touches, to make what you say wholly from your heart.

- Some couples write joint vows, which can be a lovely way to start your life together.

Notes

Traditions

Many of the traditions we know and love are very ancient. Folk believed they warded off evil spirits, and brought luck and fertility to the happy couple.

THE WHITE DRESS

The white dress symbolises purity. Many couples live together before marrying, so 'virginal' white may not apply. Instead, it can symbolise the purity of the love each bride has for her partner.

THE WEDDING RING

Romans believed that the vein in the ring finger (the fourth finger) on the left hand ran directly to the heart. And of course, the heart is the seat of love. Because of this, they called that vein the "vena amoris" or vein of love. Placing the ring on the fourth finger signifies the love that the newly married couple shares. The ring is an unbroken circle symbolising the eternal continuity of love from God and between you and your partner.

THE VEIL

This is a very old tradition. The bride wears the veil over her face to ward off evil spirits.

The veil completes the beautiful and romantic image of the blushing bride. However, many brides opt for a flower crown or hair jewels.

Traditions continued

Something old, something new, something borrowed, something blue.

SOMETHING OLD
Symbolises continuity with the past. Our lives are shaped by people from the past. Philosophers believe that the past, present and future are all connected.

SOMETHING NEW
Symbolises new beginnings and trust in the future.

SOMETHING BORROWED
From someone who is happily married, so the good luck will be shared by the couple. It also reminds them that friends and family will be there for support in times of need.

SOMETHING BLUE
Symbolizes purity, fidelity and love.

THE CEREMONY: THE ENTRANCE
Never mind what tradition dictates! What works for you is what is important.
You can walk down the aisle together - or separately.
Dads can be involved - or mums - or not!
Whatever you choose, savour the magic of the moment!

Traditions continued

THE EXIT OF THE COUPLE

The newly married couple exit first, followed by bridesmaids and pageboys, the chief bridesmaid, and then parents, and other members of the bridal party.

TAKING YOUR PARTNER'S NAME

Feminists say taking a partner's name is a throwback to the days when women were treated like possessions, had no rights or standing except as an addition to the man's status. Those days are long gone. What matters to you both, as individuals and as a couple, is all that really matters.

Traditions continued

Order of Speeches

As with everything to do with your wedding, these can be completely changed
to make them personal to YOUR day.

FIRST

The Fathers of the Brides welcome the guests, and toast the happy couple.

SECOND

The one of the couple (or both) responds by thanking their parents. They also thank those involved
in organising the wedding, and there is a toast to the bridesmaids.

THIRD

The Chief Bridesmaid then answers on behalf of the bridesmaids and provides some light-hearted
musings on the day and the couple. She may read emails or messages from people who haven't been
able to attend, and then offer a toast to absent friends. This can be particularly important if
significant family members have died.

Notes

....

....

....

....

....

....

....

....

....

....

Readings

Whether you are having a religious ceremony or not, readings for weddings are integral and can add something that is profound and beautiful. For a church wedding, you will need to choose a religious reading, and can then choose another that is non-religious.

I have included some of the most beautiful readings to help you.

Love is sensing the other as a presence. Love is receiving the feelings, thoughts, and intentions of the other into your own understanding. Love is fidelity over the long haul. Without fidelity love is a puff of wind, a gust of emotion. Love is talking together about insignificant things and significant things until a few important words: words, people, have similar meanings for both of you, and you both know that this is so. Love is listening together to the pulse of what-it-means-to-be-alive, to be human, to glorify that which is sacred and enjoy it.

Ross Snyder

Blessing for a Marriage by James Dillet Freeman

'May your marriage bring you all the exquisite excitements a marriage should bring, and may life grant you also patience, tolerance and understanding. May you always need one another not so much to fill your emptiness as to help you know your fullness. A mountain needs a valley to be complete; the valley does not make the mountain less, but more; and the valley is more a valley because it has a mountain towering over it. So let it be with you and you. May you need one another, but not out of weakness. May you embrace one another, but not out of lack.

May you entice one another, but not compel one another. May you succeed in all important ways with one another, and not fail in the little graces.

May you look for things to praise, often say 'I love you!' and take no notice of small faults. If you have quarrels that push you apart, may both of you hope to have good sense enough to take the first step back. May you enter the mystery which is the awareness of one another's presence – no more physical than spiritual, warm and near when you are side by side, and warm and near when you are in separate rooms or even distant cities. May you have happiness, and may you find it making each other happy. May you have love, and may you find it loving one another!'

From Captain Corelli's Mandolin by Louis de Bernieres

Love is a temporary madness, it erupts like volcanoes and then subsides. And when it subsides you have to make a decision. You have to work out whether your root was so entwined together that it is inconceivable that you should ever part. Because this is what love is. Love is not breathlessness, it is not excitement, it is not the promulgation of promises of eternal passion. That is just being in love, which any fool can do. Love itself is what is left over when being in love has burned away, and this is both an art and a fortunate accident. Those that truly love have roots that grow towards each other underground, and when all the pretty blossoms have fallen from their branches, they find that they are one tree and not two.

"Sonnet XVII" - Pablo Neruda

I don't love you as if you were the salt-rose, topaz
 or arrow of carnations that propagate fire:
I love you as certain dark things are loved,
 secretly, between the shadow and the soul.
I love you as the plant that doesn't bloom and carries
 hidden within itself the light of those flowers,
and thanks to your love, darkly in my body
lives the dense fragrance that rises from the earth.
I love you without knowing how, or when, or from where,
I love you simply, without problems or pride:
I love you in this way because
      I don't know any other way of loving
but this, in which there is no I or you,
 so intimate that your hand upon my chest is my hand,
 so intimate that when I fall asleep it is your eyes that close

Jelaluddin Rumi (13th century mystic poet)

A moment of happiness,
you and I sitting on the verandah,
 apparently two, but one in soul, you and I.
We feel the flowing water of life here,
 you and I, with the garden's beauty
and the birds singing.
The stars will be watching us,
and we will show them
what it is to be a thin crescent moon.
You and I unselfed, will be together,
indifferent to idle speculation, you and I.
The parrots of heaven will be cracking sugar
as we laugh together, you and I.
In one form upon this earth,
and in another form in a timeless sweet land.'

An Irish Wedding Blessing

You are the star of each night,
You are the brightness of every morning,
You are the story of each guest,
You are the report of every land.
No evil shall befall you, on hill nor bank,
In field or valley, on mountain or in glen.
Neither above, nor below, neither in sea,
Nor on shore, in skies above,
Nor in the depths.
You are the kernel of my heart,
You are the face of my sun,
You are the harp of my music,
You are the crown of my company

A Traditional Handfasting Poem

These are the hands of your best friend, young and strong, holding yours on your wedding day.
These are the hands that will work alongside yours, as together you build your future and realise your dreams.
These are the hands that will hold you when fear or grief fills your mind.
These are the hands that will wipe tears from your eyes.
These are the hands that will help you to hold your family as one.
These are the hands that will give you strength when you need it.
And lastly, these are the hands that, even when aged, will always be reaching for yours: today, tomorrow and forever.

Erin Lawless

We, unaccustomed to courage
 exiles from delight
 live coiled in shells of loneliness
 until love leaves its high holy temple
 and comes into our sight
 to liberate us into life.

Love arrives
and in its train come ecstasies
old memories of pleasure
ancient histories of pain.
Yet if we are bold,
love strikes away the chains of fear
from our souls

We are weaned from our timidity
In the flush of love's light
we dare be brave
And suddenly we see
that love costs all we are
and will ever be.
Yet it is only love
which sets us free

Touched by an Angel by Maya Angelou

Notes

Photo courtesy www.wringworthy.co.uk

Your DIY Wedding

Your style, your choice

Post Covid, couples are looking for a unique and personal experience that is meaningful for them. , rather than the 'one-size-fits-all' model' So there is an increasing trend for planning a DIY wedding. Is this for you?

TOP TIPS

Do your research into what is possible and practical for you.

Advantages

- You are in control of your budget. No sneaky add-ons that ratchet up your costs.
- Your style, your choice. Anything goes – not the standard, one-size fits all package.
- Flowers and venue décor – all do-able to suit you. You can include family and friends who have creative flair to help.

Disadvantages

- Time management and keeping on top of the organising. Don't underestimate how long wedding tasks take. You need to allocate time to research what you are making, time to buy the items, making the items, and assembling on the day. Before you think about DIY-ing your wedding, consider your time and your talents.
- Having to clear up after your big day

Questions to ask

- What does your venue include in their dry-hire package?

- Will you be given adequate time before and after the wedding day to prepare and then take everything down afterwards?

- Do they have recommended suppliers?

- Will they accept and direct deliveries for you?

- Do they have provision for DJ kit and sufficient power points?

- Do they have wifi?

- Do they have tap water available (for flower vases etc)

- Does your venue have a bar and staff that will be available?

- Does your caterer provide a waiter service?

What to add to your planning list and source

- Ordering/buying flowers and delivery
- Table and chair hire (if not provided by the venue)
- Crockery hire
- Cutlery hire
- Glassware hire
- Wine, champagne
- Table cloths and napkins hire (if not provided by the venue)
- Table décor – vases, containers, table runners
- Dance floor for an outdoor wedding
- Mobile toilets if you are having a tepee wedding and they are not provided by the venue. Don't forget toilet supplies and disposal of sanitary products
- Insurance

Can you DIY some aspects but not others? Absolutely!
Work out what is do-able without stress, and use suppliers for the rest

Notes

'You are the sky. Everything else is just the weather'

Pema Chodron

Micro Weddings

Definition: A micro wedding is planned for up to 20 guests attending

It can be a relaxed, magical and happy day, with those special intimate touches that are personal to you both, and that you may not be able to afford with a big wedding.

Advantages

- Costs are considerably less overall. Which means that you can spend any savings in your wedding budget on making the details more lavish, or reallocate the funds – for example, towards your honeymoon, a big first anniversary party or home improvements.
- You can concentrate on what is most important for you both, keeping traditions that have particular meaning for you and dropping others that may be 'expected' in a big wedding.
- Limiting your guest list means you are inviting only those you care about most and who care about you! Availability is likely to be easier to work out. And you will be able to greet and speak to everyone for more than a few minutes on the big day.

BUDGET TIP
Identify your top priorities that are must-haves – like a videographer and photographer, outdoor setting, dream wedding cake and so on.

Notes

Wedding Insurance

Is it worth buying?

Generally, the advice is – yes. But with people feeling the pinch because of the consequences of the pandemic, couples are going to be much more savvy about who and what they pay for. Couples are looking at what is really important to them, and making their choices accordingly.

Here are the main points.....

- Check your budget. Could you comfortably afford to rearrange everything if something went wrong and you have to cancel everything and reschedule?
- If rearranging things will not cause too much hassle for you, then insurance may be an unnecessary outlay.
- If you pay by credit card, you have some protection, especially for goods bought. But personal crises, like accident and illness, are not included and that's where insurance is a better option.

What does it cover? The unexpected!

According to www.moneysavingsexpert.com, wedding insurance generally covers the following:
- Your venue cancels (this may include an outbreak of infection at the venue, but NOT government dictat)
- A supplier lets you down
- Key people unexpectedly cannot attend due to accident, illness or death (this won't include pre-existing conditions)
- Important items are lost, stolen or damaged – the dress, rings, outfits, gifts and so on.
- Photos and videos don't turn up
- Personal liability and legal expenses

However, there are all sorts of aspects that are not covered and you need to make sure you are fully informed before you get out your credit card. Sounds like a no brainer but make sure you read the small print, and that anything that is unclear or sounds ambiguous is confirmed in writing.

Some experts still feel that, despite everything, wedding insurance should be an integral factor of any wedding plans.

As a first step check www.compareweddinginsurance.org.uk

Notes

Your Budget

These are the average spending allocations for the main areas of a wedding

- Venue and Catering: 40%
- Photography and Videography: 15%
- Wedding Attire and Beauty: 5%
- Music/Entertainment: 10%
- Flowers: 10%
- Favours and Gifts: 2%
- Transportation: 3%
- Stationery, including invitations, orders of service, menus, place cards: 3% of your budget. Average spend for invitations is around £300. Variable according to style and number.
- Cake: 2%
- Décor: 10%

Of course, these are broad averages. YOU decide how much you want to spend in any particular area.

Having a figure in mind when you speak to your suppliers can help focus the conversation, and saves dismay and disappointment when the final quote comes through.

Your Budget continued

Fees

You will also need to factor in fees, like charges for the Marriage Registration, Notice of Intent to marry, reservation of your church or temple, Registrar, minister or celebrant's fees.

Here are some examples:

Registrar fees   £46 (at Registry Office) £86 at another venue
Celebrant fees start at around   £650.

There are also fees for getting married in church. The Methodist Church, Scottish Episcopal Church, the United Reformed Church and the Quakers in Britain all welcome same-sex marriages. Check with your preferred church as to the fees they will charge and what they cover.

Possible extras: Organist, choir, bell ringers, Verger to make sure the church is clean and ready, additional heating, church flowers
Other faiths will have different charging levels.

Your Budget continued

Other incidental costs

- Insurance

- Postage for invitations and RSVP cards

- Meals and refreshments for suppliers like photographer and entertainers

- Corkage charged by the venue if you wish to bring your own wine and champagne

- Overnight accommodation if not included in your venue's package

- Breakfast the day after at your venue – check if it's included

- Wedding dress cleaning plus special storage box

- Hair and beauty trials – are they included in your stylists' deals?

- Dress and/or suit alterations

Your Budget continued

Top Tips on keeping track

Expect to exceed your initial budget figure!

- Be aware that with all the shiny cute things that are available, those little extras that add your own special touch, plus unexpected costs, your initial budget figure might get stretched or exceeded. Having an absolute upper limit can help you keep on track.
- Make your life as easy as possible!
- Having a money tracker is a great way of making sure that you're not over spending.
- Using an Excel spreadsheet or Google Docs is an easy way to record details like suppliers' details, deposits, instalments, loan repayments and so on.
- Prefer pen and paper? A ledger may be old school but works well as an on-the-spot record of outgoings
- Some sites offer a wedding budget planning app. Find the best one for you, check their charges and sign up if it all works to make your life easier.

Bank accounts

- Open a separate bank account for your wedding saving and spending.
- Once you have agreed contracts and charges with your suppliers, set up standing orders for regular payments.
- Use your favourite calendar app, diary, scheduler to record when the last payment is due and cancel the standing order on time.

Notes

Notes

Managing Stress

Planning your wedding is fun, exciting, nerve wracking – and can be incredibly stressful! Here are some ways to help you take care of you. Remember it's okay to take a step back sometimes and put the planning on pause .....

- Low energy levels can result in low mood and exhaustion. Try to avoid sitting at your desk munching as you work. Taking a break is refreshing.
- Cultivate kindly habits for each evening – going for a run, relaxation meditation, reading in bed away from screens.
- Use a journal to express your feelings – good, bad and indifferent! It's where you can safely say the unsayable when you need to, and take pleasure in and celebrate those unexpected wins and small joys that you experience.
- Self Care list: Make a list of all those things that bring you peace, comfort, happiness. This can include walking, going to the gym, having a regular massage, anything creative, reading. It doesn't have to be written down, but it will make up a handy part of your toolbox to cope with those low days and moments when your mojo seems to have shuffled off.
- Identify YOUR place. This can be a spot in your garden, a favourite park bench, a room in your house, your shed, or your whole house. It's a place where you can connect with YOU. That quiet place where you find healing, comfort and peaceful reflection, to do what you need to do for YOU in that moment.
- Be aware of your partner. There are two of you in this! Stress and overwhelm affects everyone differently – so if you notice the signs, reach out with love and kindness. Take a break together.

Notes

Notes

Your Planning Timeline

This is based on an average planning scheme of 18 months to 2 years. If you want to get married in a shorter time period, this will still work but with weeks between each stage rather than months.

Step One: 18 Months

Rough list of guests to decide size of wedding and how much you are prepared to spend.

Assess your savings plans, current commitments, loan options and so on.
TIP: Have a preferred maximum, plus an absolute maximum. Work on the first while keeping the second in reserve.

Decide your wedding party:
Chief Bridesmaid, bridesmaids, flowergirls, ushers

Discuss and decide on your style of wedding: barn, tepee, hotel venue, castle or stately home, DIY etc.

View, select and provisionally book venue.

Contact Minister/Registrar to check availability, plus availability of church/temple. Provisionally book.

Buy wedding insurance.

Notes

Your Planning Timeline continued

Step Two: 12 Months

Book Registrar/Minister and register intention to marry. Book celebrant if using

Book organist and choir, if having

Send out Save the Date cards

Set up wedding email account for guests and suppliers to use

Shopping for your outfit and for bridesmaids

Suppliers to book

Photographer and videographer
DJ/entertainment
Caterer
Florist
Event stylist (if using)
Wedding Cars

Notes

Your Planning Timeline continued

Step Three: 10 months

Find and book cake maker

Book honeymoon suite and overnight accommodation for guests

Finalise details with your florist and event stylist

DIY – start ordering décor items and allocating 'creating' times

Make a list of recommended hotels nearby that can provide accommodation for you and guests if your wedding venue doesn't offer this.

Decide on your ceremony details

Entrance and exit music
Readings – religious and non-religious
Vows
Photographer/videographer (check with church minister what they are allowed to do)

Decide on your Wedding Gift list
if you're having one

Order Stationery and invitations

Book honeymoon or minimoon

Notes

Your Planning Timeline continued

Step Four: 6 months

Send out invitations if you haven't already sent Save the Date cards
Book hair stylist and makeup artist
Order your rings
Purchase accessories – shoes, hair accessories, perfume, jewellery, lingerie etc

Step Five: 4 months

Start creating any DIY items

Finalise cake details

Book in menu tasting day at your venue

Work out the Timings of your day

From when to start getting ready to the time of your ceremony, reception drinks, wedding breakfast and cutting of the cake, everything needs to be laid out ready to inform your suppliers and create orders of service (if you haven't already).

Notes

Your Planning Timeline continued

Step Six: Two months

Chase any guests who haven't responded to invitations
Outfit fitting
Buy wedding party gifts
Hen party
Extra details: favours, guest book, welcome signs, cake knife ....
Anything that you fancy. Watch your budget!

Step Seven: One month

Pay final balances to suppliers
Send timings of the day to suppliers
Wedding playlist to your DJ
Break in new shoes
Final beauty appointments: pampering, manicure, facial.....

Make sure Chief Bridesmaid, and other members of your wedding party (don't forget parents and family) know the timings of the day, ceremony details, venue location etc

Finalise your seating plan and send to your caterer and venue, with final headcount, dietary requirements, any special access needed etc

Finalise shot list with your photographer

Timings of the day to your wedding car provider

Final fitting of dress/outfit

Notes

Timing of the Big Day

	Start time
Hair Stylist	....
Make Up Artist	....
Getting dressed	....
Photographer	....
Flowers arrive	....
Bridal party photos	....
Depart for ceremony	....

Timing of the Big Day

The Reception

Time

Depart ceremony for venue ....

Arrive at venue ....

Canapes and champagne with guests ....

Sit down for wedding breakfast ....

Meal ....

Speeches ....

Dancing ....

Couple leave venue/reception ....

Notes

Here are your checklists
and Money Tracker

Checklists

Wedding outfits

Dress and Veil

Supplier

....

Cost

....

Fitting date

....

Deposit paid

....

Final Payment and due date

....

Delivery/Collection Date and time

....

Suit

Supplier

....

Cost

....

Fitting date

....

Delivery/Collection Date and time

....

Checklists

Shoes

Supplier

....

Cost

....

....

....

....

Hairstylist

Booked

....

Deposit paid

....

Trial date

....

Final payment due

....

Checklists

Make Up Artist

Booked

....

Deposit paid

....

Trial date

....

Final payment due

....

Manicure (s)

Booked (date and time)

....

Paid

....

....

Accessories

Cost

....

Checklists

Bridesmaids and Flowergirls

Outfits

Supplier

....

Cost

....

Contract signed (if applicable)

....

Deposit Paid

....

Final Payment Due

....

Checklists

The Rings

Supplier (s)

....

Cost

....

Deposit Paid

....

Final fitting

....

Collection Date

....

Wedding Cars

Supplier

....

Cost

....

Contract signed

....

Deposit Paid

....

Final Payment

....

Checklists

The Venue

Booked

....

Cost

....

Deposit Paid

....

Contract signed

....

Name and contact detals
of Wedding Coordinator

....

Registrar/Minister/Celebrant

Booked

....

Cost/Fees

....

Contract signed (for Celebrant)

....

Paid

....

Checklists

Caterer

Supplier

....

Booked

....

Cost

....

Deposit Paid

....

Contract signed

....

Final Payment

....

DJ/Entertainment

Supplier

....

Cost

....

Contract signed

....

Deposit Paid

....

Final Payment

....

Checklists

Florist

Supplier

....

Booked

....

Cost

....

Deposit Paid

....

Contract signed

....

Final Payment

....

Photographer/Videographer

Supplier

....

Cost

....

Contract signed

....

Deposit Paid

....

Final Payment

....

Checklists

Stationery and Invitations

Supplier

....

Ordered

....

Cost

....

Deposit Paid

....

Contract signed

....

Final Payment

....

Delivery Date

....

Wedding Insurance

Supplier

....

Cost

....

Expiry Date

....

Checklists

Readings Chosen

Non-Religious

....

Reader

....

Religious

....

Reader

....

Music for Ceremony

Entrance Music

....

Exit of the Couple

....

Signing of the Marriage Document

....

....

Organist and Choir Booked

....

Fees Paid

....

The Extras

Your gifts to

Parents

Item(s) ....

Supplier ....

....

Cost ....

Chief Bridesmaid

Item (s)

....

Supplier (s)

....

Cost

....

Date Paid

....

Bridesmaids

Items
....

Supplier (s) ....

Cost ....

The Extras

Anything else?

Incidentals, or people you particularly want to thank outside your bridal party.

Use this space to note who, what and how much

....

....

....

....

....

....

....

....

Notes

Money Tracker

Your Budget Targets

	Budget	Actual Cost
Dress / Outfit		
Veil (s)		
Shoes		
Accessories		
Hair Stylist		
Make Up Artist		
Manicure		
Bridesmaids' Dresses		
The Rings		
Venue		
Caterer		

Money Tracker

Your Budget Targets

	Budget	Actual Cost
DJ/Entertainment		
Cake		
Flowers		
Event Stylist		
Registrar/Minister's Fees		
Other Fees		
Photographer/Videographer		
Wedding Cars		
Gifts		
Insurance		
Extras (favours, guest book, bunting, accommodation etc)		

Money Tracker

Your Budget Targets

	Budget	Actual Cost
Hen Do		
Anything Else		
Total Budget Target		
Actual Total Spend		

When someone else's happiness
is your happiness,
that is love

Lana Del Ray

Notes

Notes

Notes

Notes

Notes

Wishing you both .....

a wonderful day ....

with joy and happiness for all the days to come

Susan Wilde

MALDEN & WILDE

Unique Silk Floral Design

Acknowledgements

My grateful thanks go to

Kerry Ashby of www.kerryashbycoaching.com
who told me I could

The Contributors

Maisie Darling Bridal
www.maisiedarlngbridal.co.uk

Lorna's Salon
www.facebook.com/Lornassalon

Simply Irresistible Cakes London
www.simplyirresistiblecakes.com

Emma Drew Batty
www.emmadbphotography.com

Printed in Poland
by Amazon Fulfillment
Poland Sp. z o.o., Wrocław

26258269R00112